HOW DO I KNOW?

Questions & Answers About the Senses

By Robert Carola
Illustrated by Mel Crawford

Cover by Stuart Trotter

GALLERY BOOKS
An Imprint of W. H. Smith Publishers Inc.
112 Madison Avenue
New York City 10016

What are my senses?

Your senses are all the parts of your body that tell you what's happening around you. For instance, you see with your eyes, hear with your ears, feel with your skin, taste with your tongue, and smell with your nose. All of your senses work together with your brain to let you know what's going on outside your body.

What controls my senses?

The control center of all your senses—taste, smell, sight, hearing, touch, and balance—is your brain. For example, your eyes let light into your body, but it is your brain that actually figures out what you are seeing. Sometimes our brains are compared to computers, but that's not really so. Your brain is much smarter than a computer!

How many different colors can I see?

If you have a large set of crayons or colored markers, you're used to seeing a lot of colors. But you can see more shades of colors than you ever dreamed you could. Your eyes can tell the difference between thousands and thousands of different shades of colors!

Why do some people wear glasses?

Inside your eye is a part called the *lens*. It changes shape when you are looking at things very close (like when you read a book) or far away (like when you recognize a friend a block away). Some people, even children, have eyes whose lenses don't change shape very well. They have to wear eyeglasses, which have special lenses, so that they can see clearly.

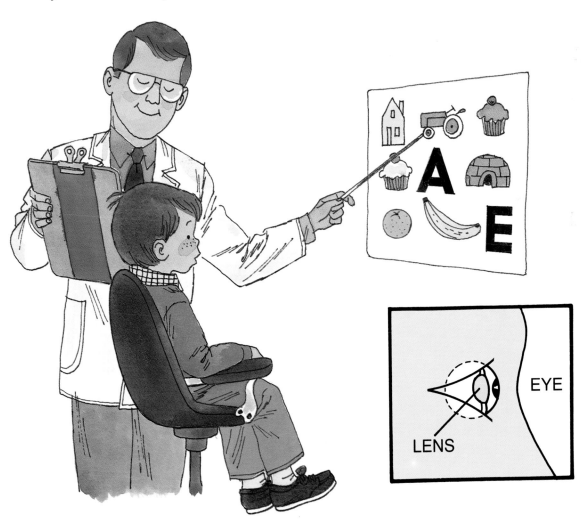

Why do people have different color eyes?

Children usually have the same color eyes as one of their parents or grandparents. Eye color is something you inherit, which means it is passed on from parents to their children. The darkness or lightness of eyes comes from something called *melanin.* The more melanin you have, the darker your eyes will be. Melanin also gives color to your skin and hair.

What color eyes do most people have?

Most people have dark-colored eyes, usually brown. Those same people usually have dark colored hair. People with blue eyes tend to have light, or blond, hair. What color eyes do you have?

How can I see in the dark?

Look in the mirror and you will see a black dot in the middle of your eye. It is called the *pupil.* It gets bigger to let in more light, or smaller to let in less light. When you walk into a dark room your pupils open wide to let in a lot of light. At the same time, special parts of your eyes called *rod cells* also help you to see in the dark. When you've been in a dark room for only a minute you can already see ten times better than when you first walked in. After 40 minutes in the dark, you can see as well as you're going to.

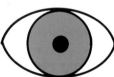

**PUPIL
IN THE LIGHT**

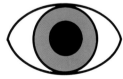

**PUPIL
IN THE DARK**

Why does it bother my eyes to look at snow on a sunny day?

On a sunny day the bright sunlight bounces off the white snow, making the light even brighter. It usually takes a while for your eyes to become comfortable when you look at something that bright. People often wear sunglasses when they go skiing or go to the beach to protect their eyes from the strong light.

Why do my eyes make tears sometimes?

You know that when you cry you make tears, but there are also other times your eyes tear. When smoke gets in your eyes or when you help Mom chop an onion, your eyes may make tears. These tears help to keep your eyes clean, and to make them feel better when something bothers them.

Why do I blink my eyes?

You blink your eyes every few seconds without thinking about it. Every time you blink a special liquid that looks like water runs across your eyes. It washes away little bits of dirt, kills germs, and keeps your eyes clear, wet, and smooth. Blinking keeps your eyes clean and healthy.

What is an optical illusion?

An optical illusion is something that tricks your eyes. You think you see one thing, but another thing is really true. For instance, which of these red lines do you think is longer?

The top one *looks* longer, doesn't it? But it's a trick. Both red lines are the same.

Here's another optical illusion. Which line is longer, the red or the black? You probably said the black line is longer, or maybe you figured out that it only *looks* longer. Actually, both lines are the same.

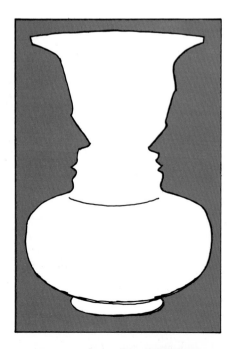

Another kind of optical illusion uses shapes instead of lines to fool your eyes. Do you see a vase or two faces? Or maybe you see both pictures? Sometimes an artist can make two different things out of one picture.

Why can something look two different ways?

Sometimes your brain helps you imagine that one thing looks like something else. Have you ever looked up at the clouds and thought you saw a face or an animal or something else? Your eyes see a cloud, but your imagination turns it into an elephant .

What is braille?

Since they cannot see, blind people use *braille* to read and write. Braille is a way of showing letters and numbers as raised dots that can be felt with the fingertips. The dots are like a special code that blind people learn to understand.

Do people with big ears hear better?

The part of your ear that is important for hearing is *inside* your ear, where you can't see it. The size of the outside part of your ear makes no difference in how well you hear.

Do I hear better than grown-ups?

Yes, you do. In fact, babies usually hear the best of all, so let's not make any really loud, scary noises if there's a baby in the room. Most grown-ups don't hear as well as children. As people get older, some of the tiny parts inside their ears may not work as well as they used to. If you take very good care of your body, your hearing probably won't change very much when you're a grown-up.

Are loud sounds bad for my ears?

Very loud sounds, if they last for a while, can harm the delicate parts inside your ears that help you to hear. People who work near airplanes at an airport, or who work with noisy machines, wear special ear coverings to protect their hearing.

Why do children's voices sound smaller than adult voices?

Inside your throat are folds of skin called *vocal cords.* We don't have to think about it, but we make sounds by pulling the vocal cords together and letting air from the chest come up and pass over them. Your vocal cords are shorter and thinner than a grown-up's, so your voice sounds smaller than a grown-up's voice.

Why do I sound different on tape?

When you listen to yourself talk, your voice is changed a little bit. Some of the sound you are hearing is carried through the bones of your head. It's almost like when your voice sounds louder in an empty room. When you hear yourself on tape, your voice is carried only by the air, and it sounds the way it always sounds to other people.

Why do I get dizzy sometimes?

You usually get dizzy when you spin around quickly, and then suddenly stop. When you stop, a liquid inside your ear keeps moving. The moving liquid makes you feel like you are still moving, but in the other direction. Your brain gets a little mixed up by all this, and you feel dizzy for a little while.

Why do my ears "pop"?

You may have heard of the *eardrum,* a thin piece of skin between the inner and outer parts of your ear. Usually, the air pressing on your eardrum is the same on both sides, and you can't feel it. But when you're in an airplane that's taking off or landing, or in an elevator in a tall building, the force of the air pressing on your eardrum may change all of a sudden. You feel that change because it makes your ears "pop." You can usually feel better right away by swallowing, or opening your mouth wide as though you were yawning.

What does my tongue do?

Your tongue does lots of things. It has little bumps on it called "taste buds." They allow you to taste the difference between salty food like potato chips and sweet food like candy or ice cream. Your tongue helps you chew your food by moving the food to where your teeth can bite it. After your food is all chewed up, your tongue helps to push it down your throat to your stomach. And here's something *very* important about your tongue—it helps you to talk. Just try to say "hello" or "goodbye" without moving your tongue!

Do I taste food better than grown-ups do?

You certainly do taste food better than grown-ups do,
because you have more taste buds that work. As you get
older, some taste buds get worn out and don't work anymore.

Why does my mouth water when I see something good to eat?

The watery liquid in your mouth is called *saliva.* Because saliva is so important in helping you digest your food, you start making extra saliva (your mouth begins to "water") as soon as you see or smell something good to eat. By the time you actually start eating the food you have plenty of saliva ready to do its job!

Why can't I taste food when I have a cold?

When you taste food you are actually tasting it *and* smelling it at the same time. If you can't smell your food, you can't taste it either. Try holding your nose and eating a piece of food. Could you taste it? If you have a cold, you probably have a stuffy nose too, and you can't taste your food very well because the "smellers" in your nose are blocked.

How many different smells can I smell?

Your nose is amazing—it can smell about 4,000 different smells! You probably have only three or four favorites. Perhaps it's the smell of freshly baked cookies or just-mowed grass or your mother's perfume? What is your favorite?

Why does my nose run when I cry?

You know that when you cry, tears flow out of your eyes. But they may also slide down a tube that goes from inside your eyes to your nose, and that makes your nose begin to run. That's why some people need to blow their nose when they cry.

What is my "funny bone"?

If you have ever bumped the "funny bone" near your elbow, you know it's not funny! In fact, it's not even a bone. What we call the funny bone is really a nerve. We call it "funny" because it tingles when we bump it.

Why does my foot fall asleep sometimes?

Sometimes when you cross your legs for awhile you block the blood from reaching your foot, and your foot feels numb. When you uncross your legs and let the blood go through again, you may get a tingly feeling. Why? All the little nerves that "fell asleep" because they didn't get enough blood are now waking up. You can almost feel them waking up and stretching.

Why do I get itchy sometimes?

You feel itchy, and you want to scratch, when something very light and delicate touches your skin. Tiny "feelers" in your skin called *nerve endings* send a message to your brain, and you usually end up scratching. You might also feel itchy if you have a bug bite or a rash.

Why does hot feel different from cold?

You have special nerve endings in your skin for hot or cold, light touch or heavy touch, pain, itch, and tickle. If you touch something hot, then the "hot" nerve endings send a message to your brain. If you touch something cold, then it is the "cold" nerve endings that send the message. When your brain gets the message, then you know exactly what you are touching!

Why do I use my fingertips to touch and feel things?

There are many special nerve endings in your fingertips that let you touch and feel things—even very small things. As good as your fingertips are at feeling things, they are not the best touchers and feelers in your body. Can you guess what part of your body is the best "toucher" and "feeler"? It's the tip of your tongue!

Why do I get a headache sometimes?

There are many reasons why you might get a headache. Headaches
sometimes happen when you have a cold or are not feeling well.
Sometimes your eyes get tired, maybe from watching too much
television, and you get a headache. Or you may get a headache
that's mostly in your forehead and cheeks. That's usually a *sinus*
headache. Sinuses are little empty spaces inside your head that can
get infected or can hurt when the weather changes suddenly. It's
best to rest when you have a headache.

Why can't babies talk?

Learning to talk takes time. Babies have to listen for a long time before they can copy what they hear. When they are first born, babies cry to let you know they want something. By their first birthday, they can say a few simple words. They learn to say many words and even simple sentences by the time they are two years old.

Why do I get sleepy?

Sometimes you're so busy, or you're having such a good time that you don't even realize that you're getting tired. But sooner or later, your brain always lets you feel sleepy so you'll know it's time to go to bed. Sleep is one of the most important things your body needs, and your brain helps you to stay healthy by making sure you get enough rest.

How do I know when to wake up?

If you go to bed when you are supposed to, and you're not sick or more tired than usual, you will probably wake up all by yourself in plenty of time to have breakfast. How do you do that? Everybody needs a different amount of sleep to keep healthy (grown-ups need less than you do), and your brain "knows" when you've had enough sleep. When it's time to wake up, your brain sets off a special alarm that only you can feel, and you wake up.